D0122727

Dear Parent:
Your child's love of reading starts here!

Every child learns to read in a different way and at his or her own speed. Some go back and forth between reading levels and read favorite books again and again. Others read through each level in order. You can help your young reader improve and become more confident by encouraging his or her own interests and abilities. From books your child reads with you to the first books he or she reads alone, there are I Can Read Books for every stage of reading:

SHARED READING
Basic language, word repetition, and whimsical illustrations, ideal for sharing with your emergent reader

BEGINNING READING
Short sentences, familiar words, and simple concepts for children eager to read on their own

READING WITH HELP
Engaging stories, longer sentences, and language play for developing readers

READING ALONE
Complex plots, challenging vocabulary, and high-interest topics for the independent reader

I Can Read Books have introduced children to the joy of reading since 1957. Featuring award-winning authors and illustrators and a fabulous cast of beloved characters, I Can Read Books set the standard for beginning readers.

A lifetime of discovery begins with the magical words "I Can Read!"

*Visit www.icanread.com for information
on enriching your child's reading experience.*

This book is dedicated to people who protect
North America's prairies so that herds of bison
can still run wild.
—J.B.

The National Wildlife Federation & Ranger Rick contributors: Children's
Publication Staff, Licensing Staff, and in-house naturalist David Mizejewski

Ranger Rick: I Wish I Was a Bison
Copyright © 2019 National Wildlife Federation
All rights reserved.
Manufactured in China. No part of this book may be used or reproduced in any manner whatsoever without
written permission except in the case of brief quotations embodied in critical articles and reviews. For
information address HarperCollins Children's Books, a division of HarperCollins Publishers, 195 Broadway,
New York, NY 10007.
www.icanread.com
www.RangerRick.com

Library of Congress Control Number: 2019937379
ISBN 978-0-06-243226-1 (trade bdg.)—ISBN 978-0-06-243225-4 (pbk.)

Typography by Brenda E. Angelilli
19 20 21 22 23 SCP 10 9 8 7 6 5 4 3 2 1   ❖   First Edition

Ranger Rick

I Wish I Was a Bison

by Jennifer Bové

HARPER

An Imprint of HarperCollinsPublishers

What if you wished you were a bison?

Then you became a bison calf.

Could you eat like a bison?

Bathe like a bison?

Live in a bison family?

And would you want to? Find out!

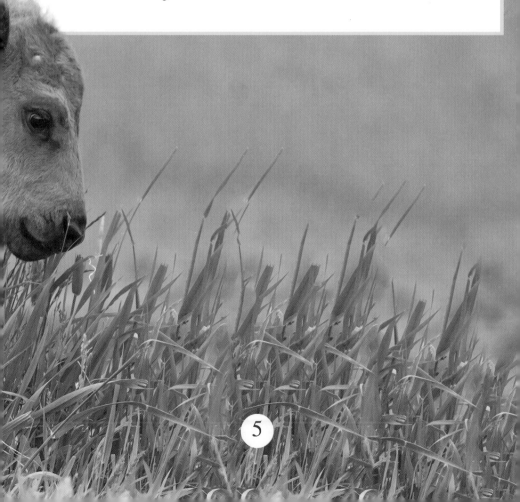

Where would you live?

Most bison live on prairies
in North America.
Prairies have grasses and flowers,
but not many trees.

Summers are hot and dry.

Winters are cold and snowy.

Bison do not stay in just one spot.

They roam all around the prairie.

What would your family be like?

Adult female bison are called cows.

Young bison are called calves.

Cows and calves live together
in groups called herds.

Adult male bison are called bulls.

Bulls live together in separate herds.

A bison mom has a calf each spring.

Calves can stand up and walk

just a few minutes after being born!

A bison calf stays near its mom

for almost a year.

It drinks her milk and cuddles

against her thick fur.

How would you talk?

Bison talk with grunts and snorts.

They also talk with their tails.

What do you do when you are angry or scared?

A bison wags its tail when it's calm. When a bison is angry or scared, its tail stands up straight.

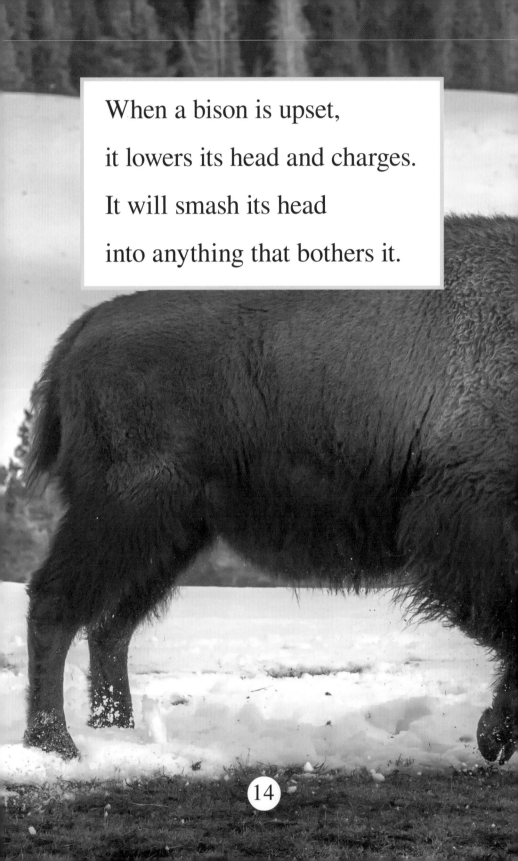

When a bison is upset,
it lowers its head and charges.
It will smash its head
into anything that bothers it.

Bison bulls will also crash
their heads together
to show who is the strongest.

15

How would you learn to be a bison?

Bison calves learn by playing.
They push their heads together
and charge each other for fun.

Bison calves love to run. Running helps them grow strong and fast.

Bison calves must be fast
to keep up with their herd.
A herd will run suddenly
to escape from wolves or bears.
This is called stampeding.

What would you eat?

Bison eat grass—

lots and lots of grass!

This is called grazing.

It is easy to graze in the summer.

In winter, bison must find grass
under deep snow.
They sweep their heads
from side to side
to move the snow off the grass.

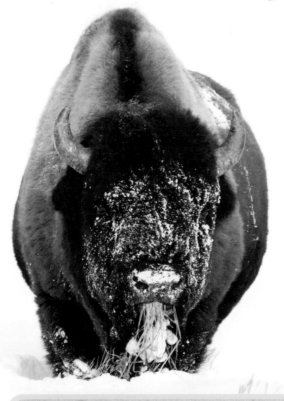

Would you like to eat the same food every day?

How would you wash up?

Bison don't use soap and water to get clean.

They take dust baths.

Rolling in the dirt helps bison get rid of bugs and shed itchy fur.

This is called wallowing.

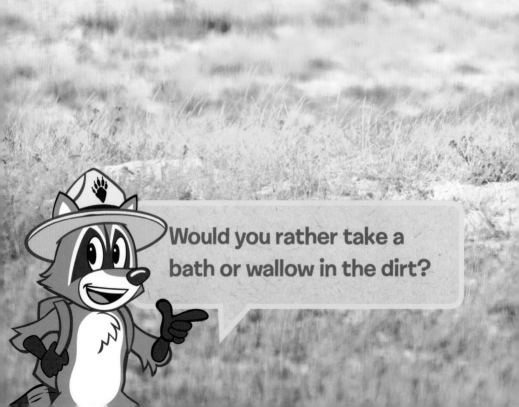

Would you rather take a bath or wallow in the dirt?

How would growing up change you?

A bison calf is born with red fur.

Within a few months,

its fur begins to grow darker.

A calf will also start to grow horns
and a hump on its shoulders.
Male bison have bigger horns
and shoulder humps than females.

After about three years,

a male calf leaves his mom's herd

to join a herd of bulls.

A female bison stays
with her mother's herd
for her whole life.
At about three years old,
she is ready to have a calf
of her own.

Being a bison could be cool.

But do you want to live in a herd?

Eat grass all day long?

Wallow in the dirt?

Luckily, you don't have to.

You're not a bison.

You're YOU!

Did You Know?

- Bison are the largest land animals in North America.

- Bison can jump six feet (1.8 meters) high. That means a bison could jump over a grown person!

- A bison's shoulder hump is full of strong muscles. It helps the bison plow its large head through snow.

- The hair hanging from a bison's chin is called a beard.

- Bison grow thick fur in winter to stay warm. In the spring, the thick fur falls off in chunks.

- President Obama signed the National Bison Legacy Act, a law that made the bison the national mammal of the United States.

- Some bison also live in Europe. They are called wisent (pronounced VEE-zent).

- Many people in North America use the term buffalo to refer to bison. But bison are not closely related to true buffalo, which are found in Africa and Asia. Bison are different than buffalo because they have shoulder humps, beards, and short horns.

Bison Frisbee

Bison eat a lot of grass—and they poop a lot, too. Their poop is very important to the prairie grasslands because it breaks down into healthy soil, and this makes more grass grow. In the 1800s, people traveling across the prairies didn't have wood to burn. So they made campfires by burning dried bison poop. Kids also used the dried poop as Frisbees! You can make a paper plate Frisbee that looks like bison poop but doesn't smell stinky.

What You Need:

- **2 paper plates** • **Paper towels or toilet paper** • **Stapler**
- **Brown and green craft paint** • **A handful of grass (optional)**

What You Do:
Place one plate on top of the other so that they are face-to-face.
Staple evenly around the edges of the plates, leaving a few inches open.
Stuff paper towels or toilet paper in the opening until the space between the plates is full.
Staple the opening closed.
Paint both sides of the Frisbee with brown and green paint. You can be messy!
Before the paint dries, press bits of grass onto the wet surface. The grass will make the dried Frisbee look very realistic.
Invite your friends over for a funny game of bison poop Frisbee.

Wild Words

Bull: an adult male bison

Calf: a baby or young bison

Charge: to run toward something

Cow: an adult female bison

Graze: to eat grass

Grunt: a low noise from a bison's throat

Herd: a group of bison

Prairie: large areas of grassy land in the central and western parts of North America

Shed: to lose fur; bison shed their thick winter coat in the spring

Stampede: to run together in a herd to escape danger

Wallow: to roll in the dirt; the dirt spot where a bison rolls is also called a wallow

Dig Deeper
WANT TO FIND OUT EVEN MORE ABOUT BISON?

Check out the Ranger Rick website: www.RangerRick.com
SEARCH: bison

Photography from the archives of National Wildlife Federation by Jeremy Mathieu. Photography copyright © Getty Images by Russell Burden, Tom Walker, Design Pics, brytta, Hal Beral, Parfenov Yuril, Jim Cumming, Daniel Viñé Garcia, Larry Gerbrandt, Patrick Caughlan, CR Courson, and Bob Pool.